Adam and Eve
by Adino Israel
illustrated by Jason Lee

Conscious Dreams

PUBLISHING

Adam and Eve

Copyright © 2023: Adino Israel

All rights reserved. No part of this publication may be produced, distributed, or transmitted in any form or by any means, including photocopying, recording, or other electronic or mechanical methods, without the prior written permission of the publisher, except in the case of brief quotations embodied in critical reviews and certain other non-commercial uses permitted by copyright law.

First Printed in United Kingdom 2023

Published by Conscious Dreams Publishing
www.consciousdreamspublishing.com

Cover design and illustrations by Jason Lee
www.jasonmation.co.uk

Edited by Daniella Blechner

ISBN: 978-1-915522-46-7

Dedication

All praises to the most-high God of Israel and His mighty son, Christ our Lord, through which come salvation, grace, mercy, and peace.

In the beginning, God first created His son Christ who He brought up and was His daily delight. Then, Christ created the 24 Elders and the Archangels and then Angels.

From the very beginning, Christ was created and given eternal life. Christ existed before God created the earth and when there were no depths to the sea. He existed before the mountains, the fields and the highest parts of the world. Before God prepared the deep space, the planets, the stars, the sky and the clouds, Christ was by God's side.

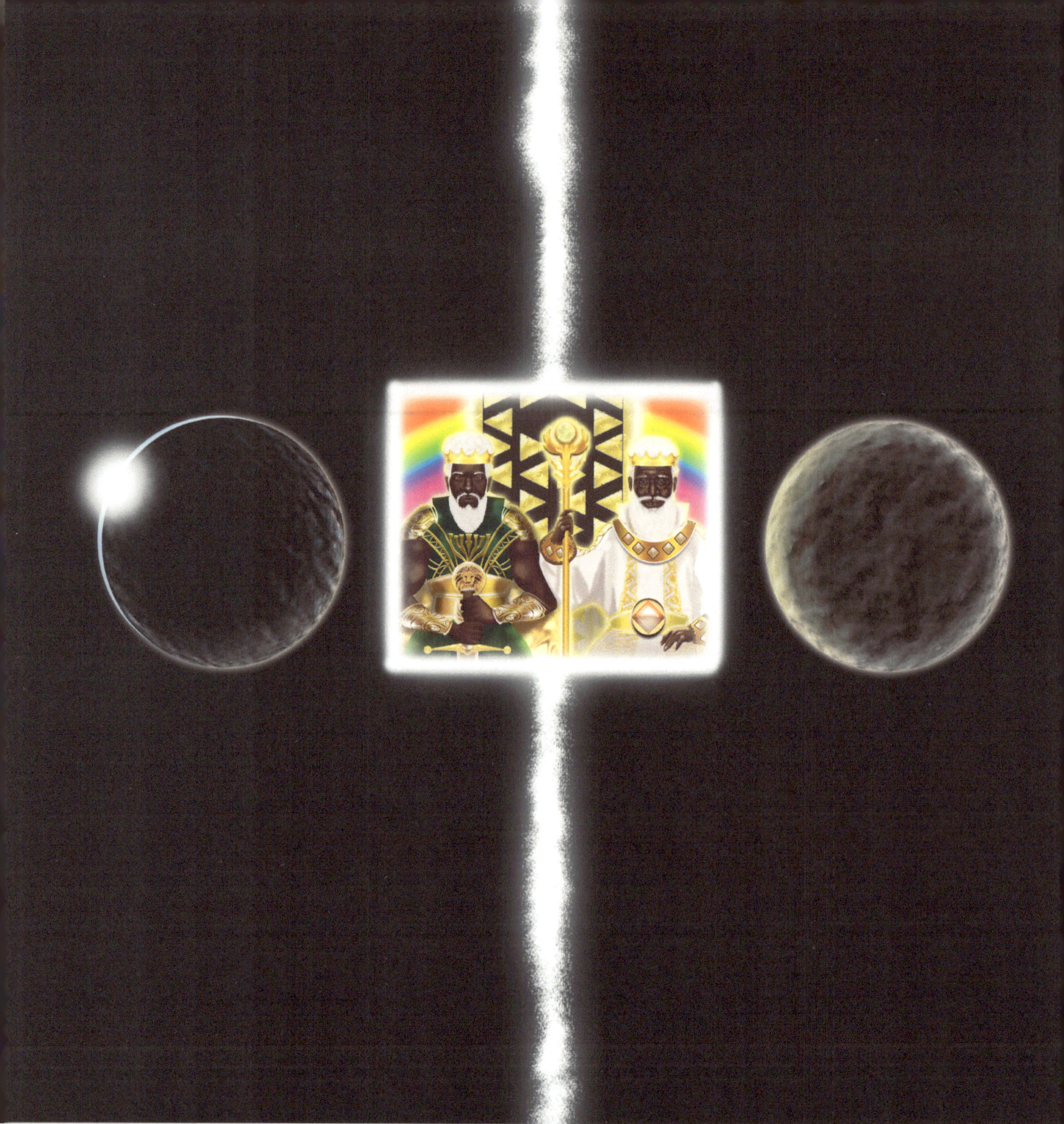

When God created the heavens and the earth, the earth was without form. It was completely empty, and darkness covered the earth. The Spirit of God was moving over the face of the waters.

God said, 'Let there be light,' and there was light upon the earth. God saw the light and that it was good. He divided the light from the darkness. He called the light 'Day' and the darkness 'Night'. Then God said, 'This is the first day.'

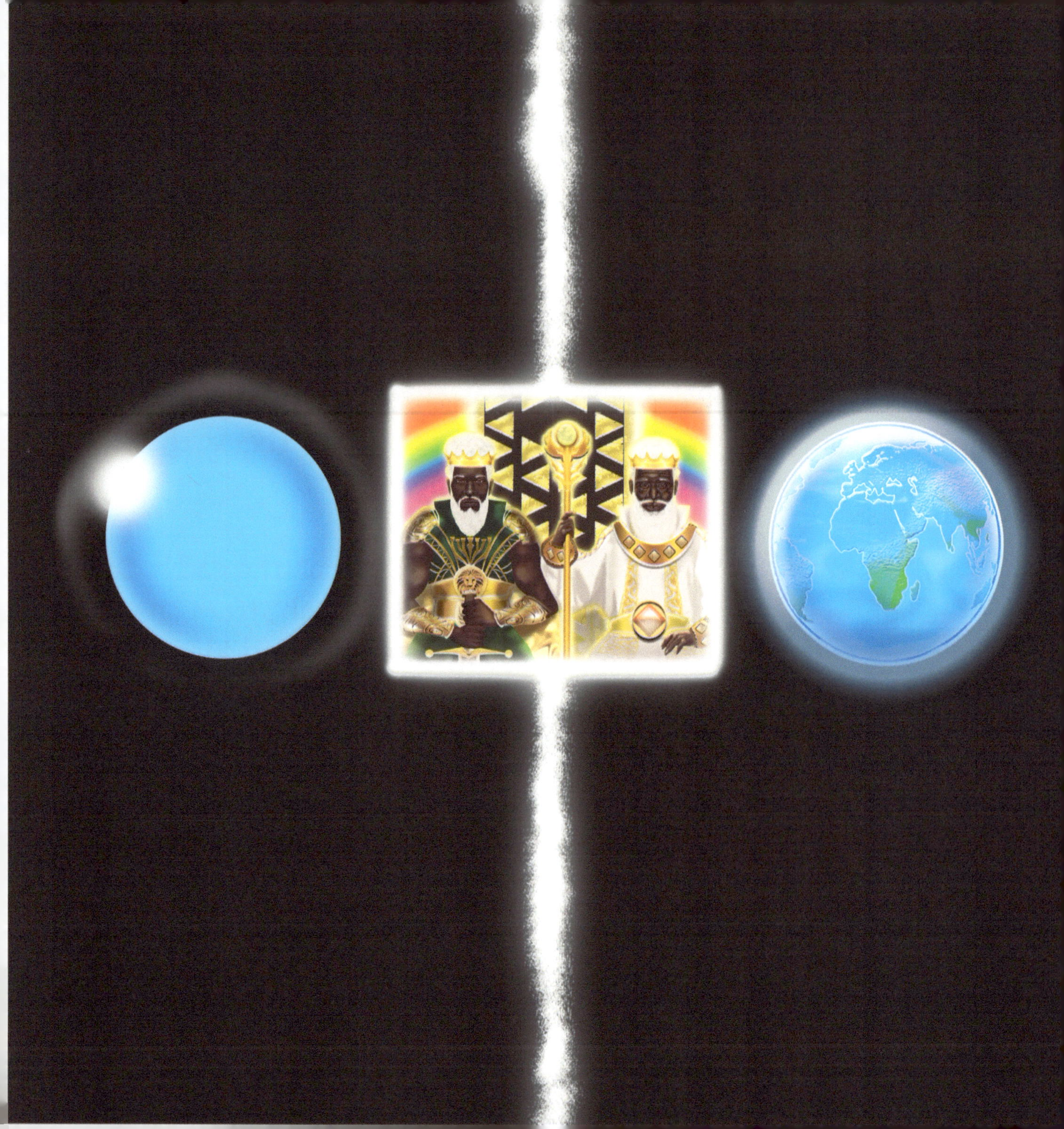

When God created The Heavens, he divided it into two parts: the deep space and the sky. God created the ozone layer between them, and God called the deep space and the sky 'The Heavens'. This was the second day.

And God said, 'Let the water under the sky be gathered together in one place and let the dry land appear.' And it was done. Then God called the dry land to come forward out of the water, which he called 'The Seas' and he saw that it was good.

Then God said, 'Let the dry land grow grass plants and fruit trees after their kind.' And God said it was good. This was the third day.

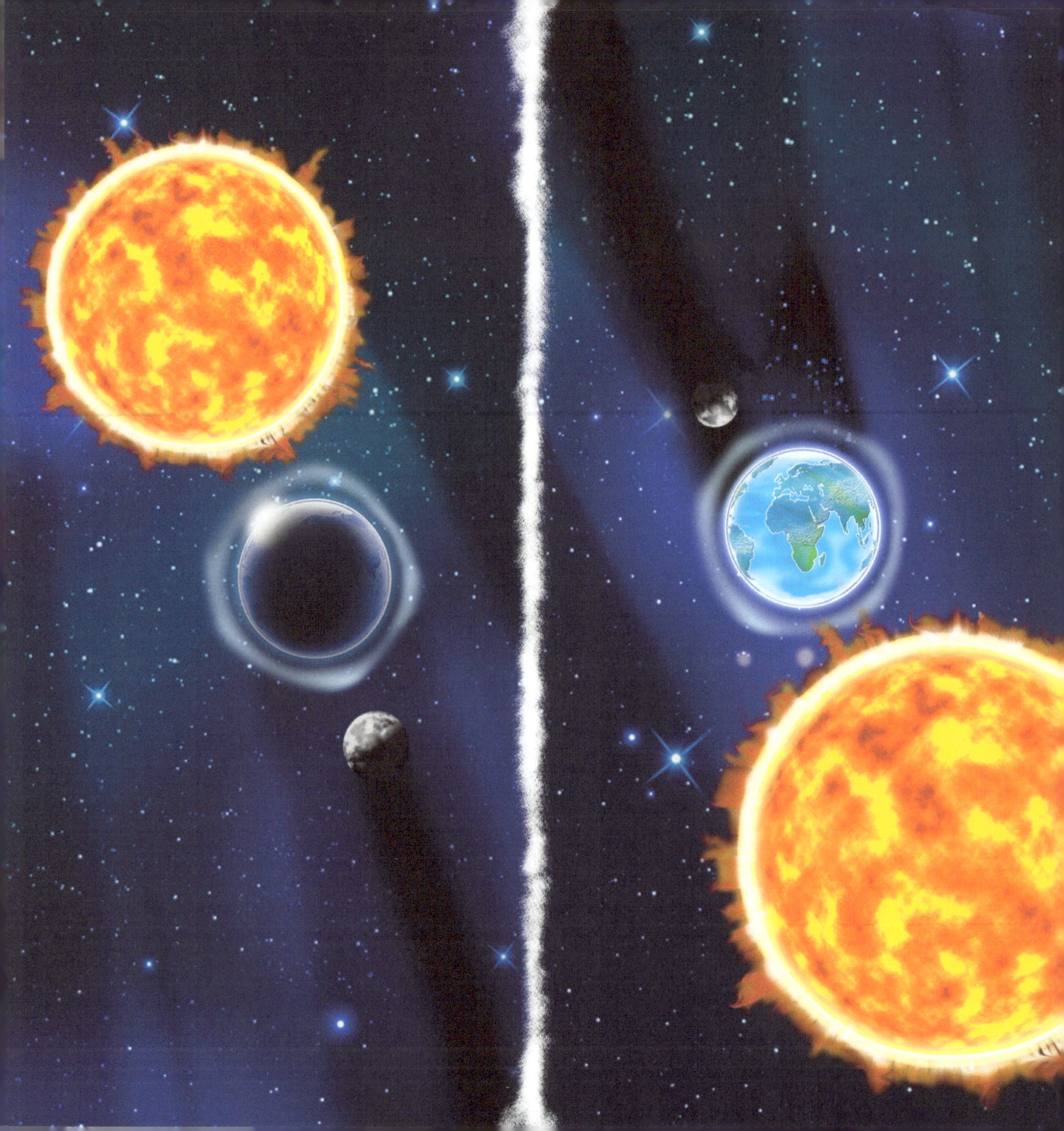

God said, 'Let there be light in the heavens to divide the day from the night; and let them be for signs and seasons, and for days and years.'

And God made two great lights: the greater light was the sun to rule the day, and lesser light, the moon to rule the night. The full moon was to count months and the years, and the sun was used to show us different seasons. This was the fourth day.

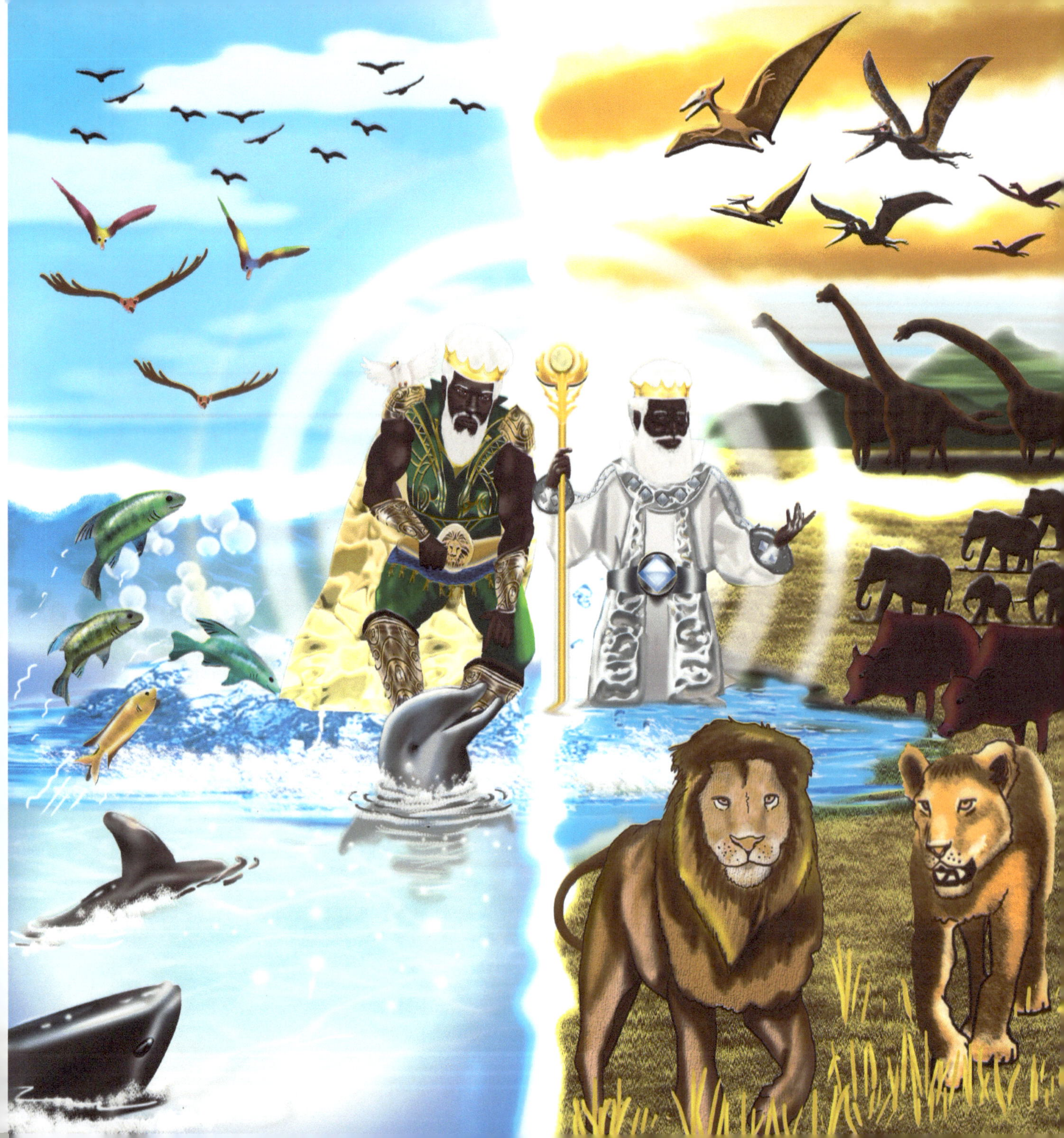

God created all the creatures in the sea and the birds that flew in the sky and God created the living creatures great and small. He created the cattle beasts and insects and all creeping things that walk on the earth. This was the fifth day.

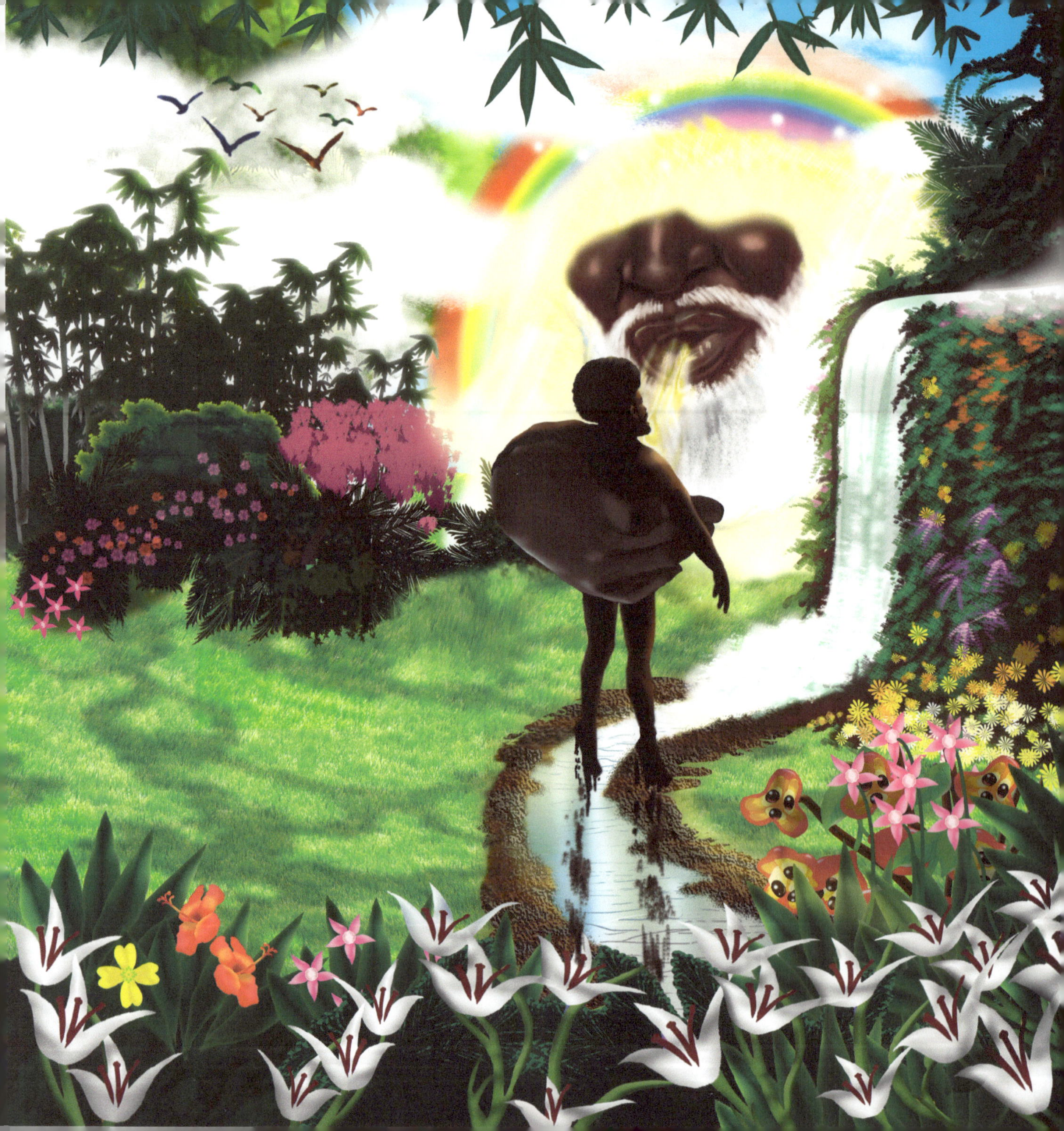

God said to Christ, 'Let us make man in Our image.' Then he gave them power and control over all creatures in the sea on the dry land and in the air. And he would make male and female.

God made man out of the dark brown soil of the ground and breathed into his nostrils the breath of life, which were God's commandments and the laws. Then the man became a living soul. And God called him Adam, which means 'from the ground.'

And God blessed him and said, 'Be fruitful and multiply.' He wanted them to have children. Then God said to both man and creatures, 'I have given you every herb bearing seed, which is upon the face of all the earth, and every tree, to you it shall be for food.' This was the sixth day.

Garden of Eden

The heavens and earth were finished. By the seventh day, God had finished all his work. He rested so He could enjoy all that He had created. God blessed the seventh day and made it a holy day.

Then God planted a garden eastward in Eden and called it the Garden of Eden. Inside the garden, He placed the man He called Adam and Adam's job was to look after the garden. God commanded Adam saying, 'Of every tree of the garden you may freely eat; but of the tree of the knowledge of good and evil you shall not eat or you shall surely die.'

God said it is not good that Adam should be alone. 'I will make him a helper comparable to him,' God said.

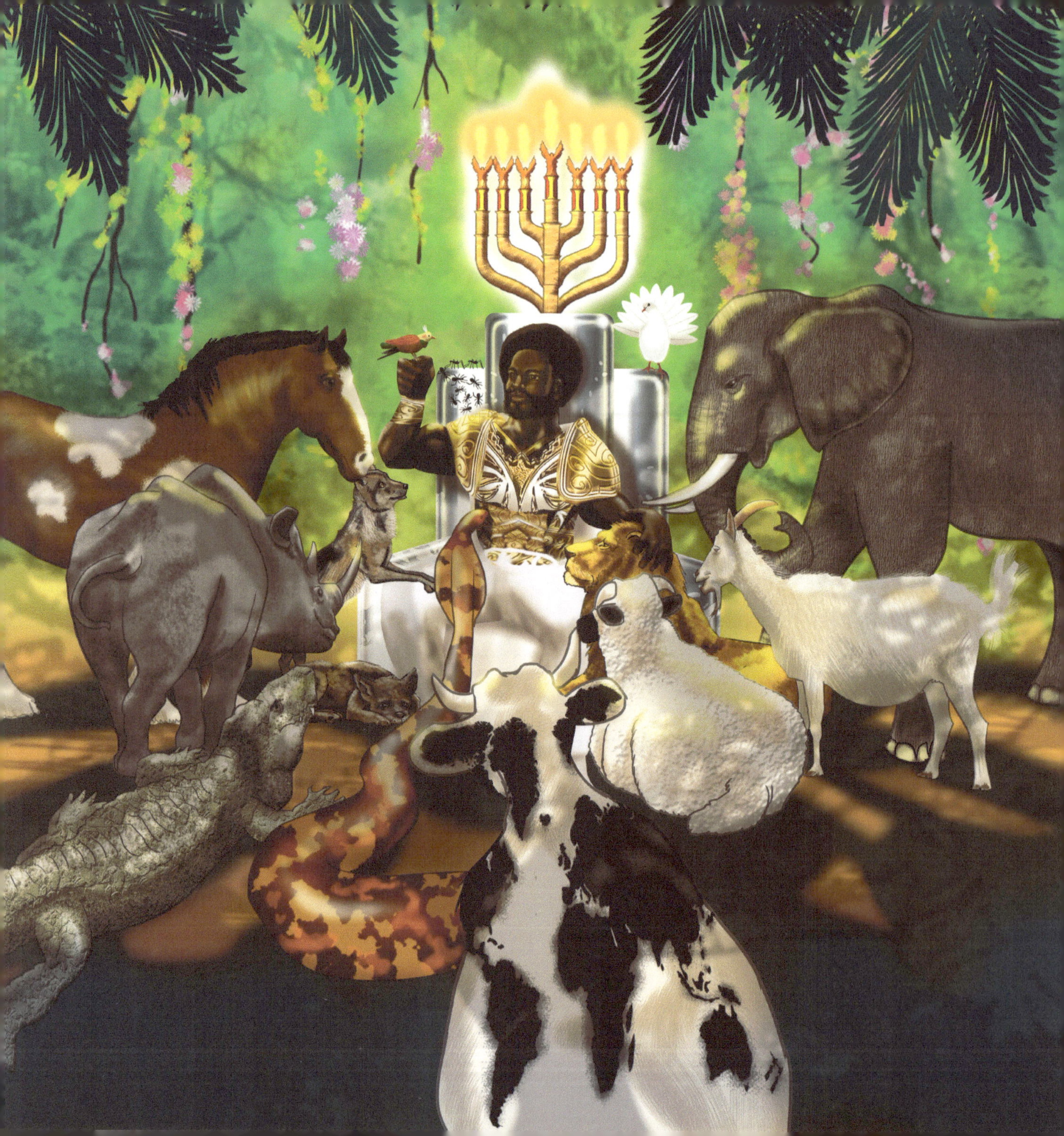

God created all the creatures from out of the ground and he brought them to Adam to see what Adam would call them, and whatever Adam called them that would be their name.

Adam gave names to all the creatures big and small in the sea and on the land and in the air, but for Adam there was no helper that looked similar to him.

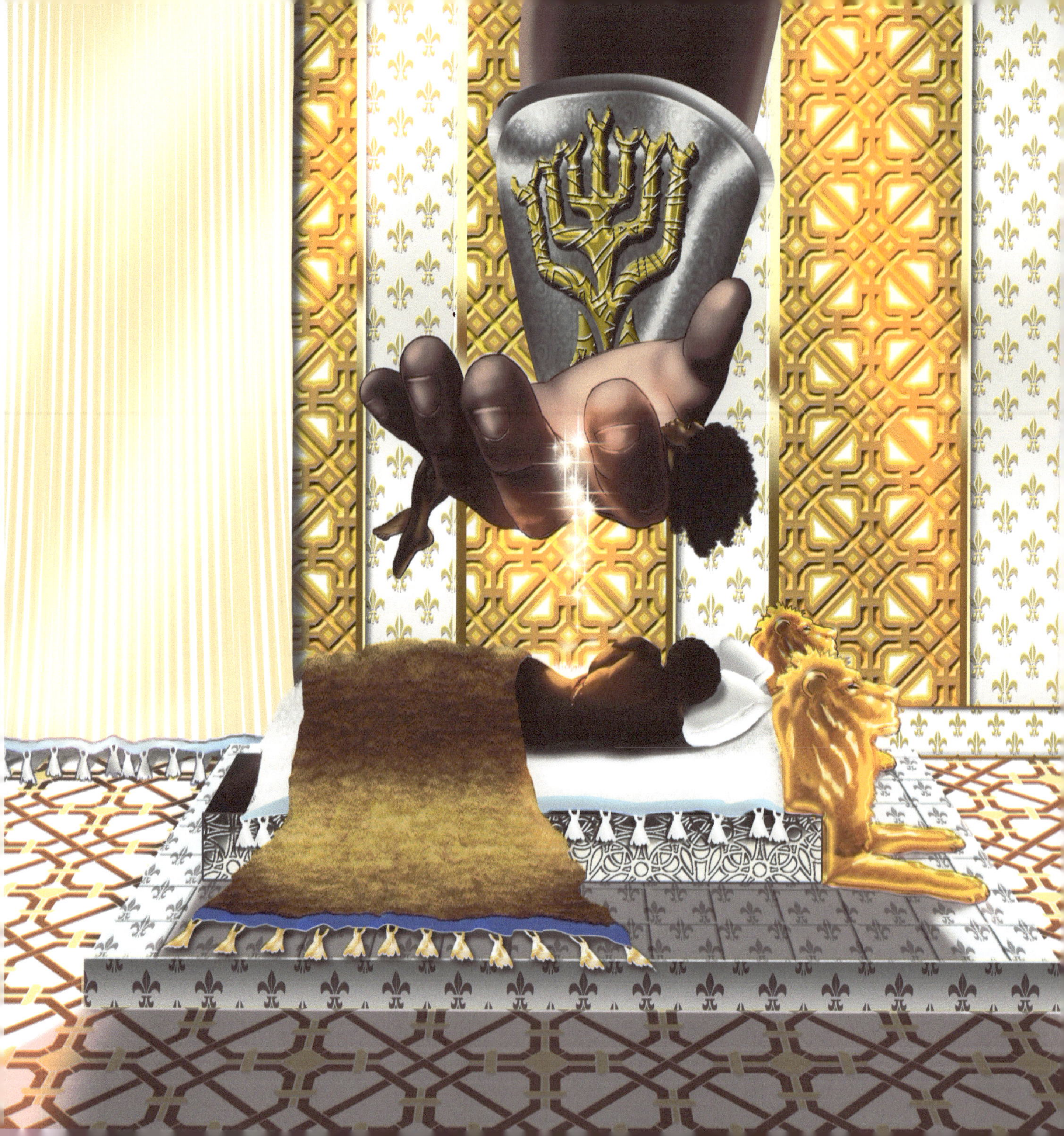

God caused a deep sleep to fall upon Adam and he slept. Then God opened Adam's side and took one of Adam's ribs and then closed it back up.

From the rib that God took from Adam, He made Adam a woman and brought her to him. When he awoke, Adam said, 'This is now bone of my bones and flesh of my flesh: She shall be called Woman because she was taken out of Man.' She was now his wife. Her name was Eve the mother of all people.

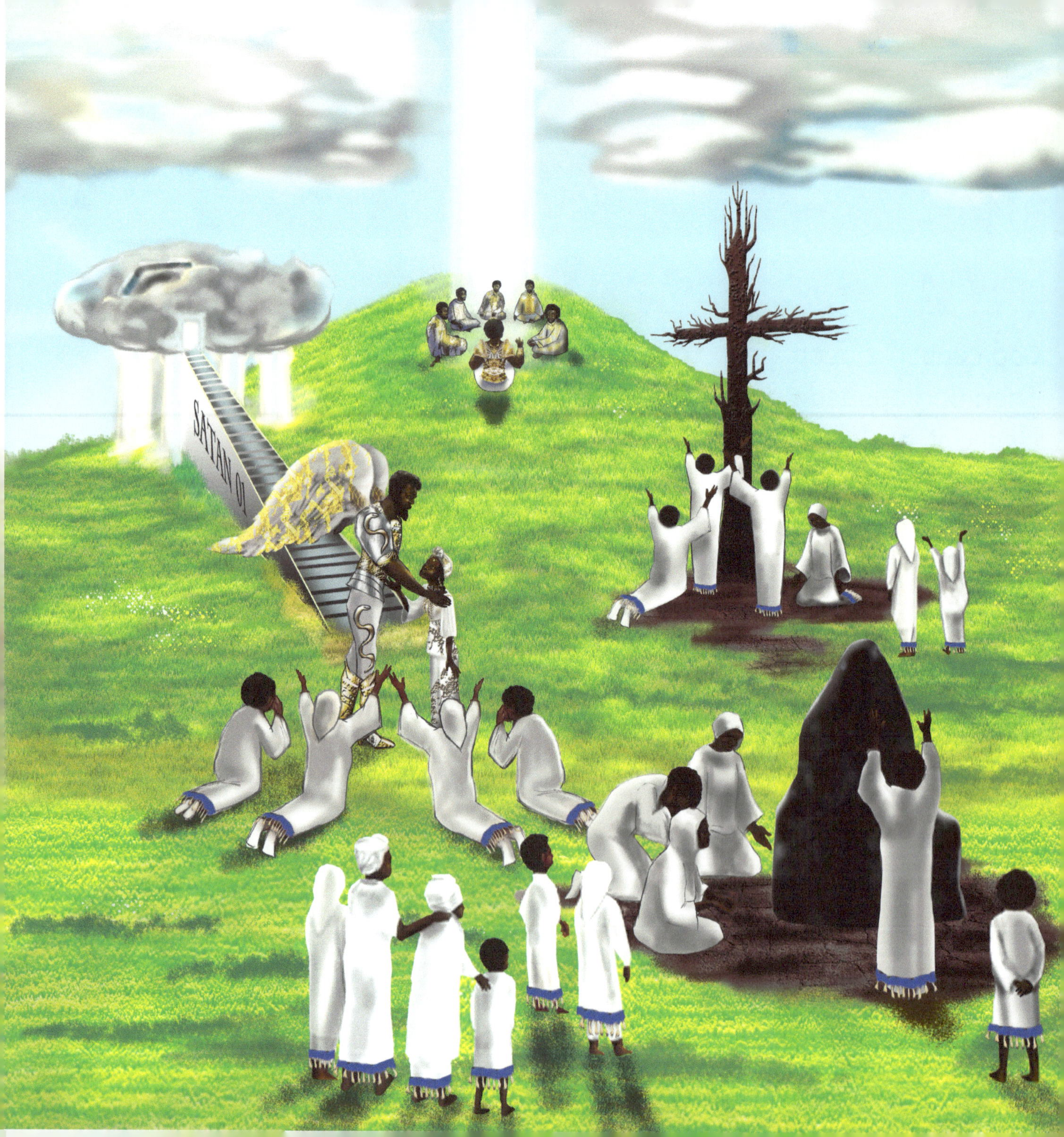
SATAN 01

Now Satan, the Devil, was the most untrustworthy creature in Eden more than any God had made. He transformed into a marvellous, good angel of light to deceive Eve.

Satan said to Eve, 'Has God indeed said, "You shall not eat of every tree in the garden"?' And Eve told Satan that they could eat from every tree except for the tree in the in the middle of the garden or they will surely die.

Satan said, 'You will not surely die. For God knows that in the day you eat of it your eyes will be opened and you will be like God, knowing good and evil.

And Eve saw that Satan was good to listen to and the tree was beautiful to look at and thought she could become wise. Eve broke God's law by learning from Satan and Eve taught Adam what she had learnt. They knew they had broken God's commandments by listening and following Satan.

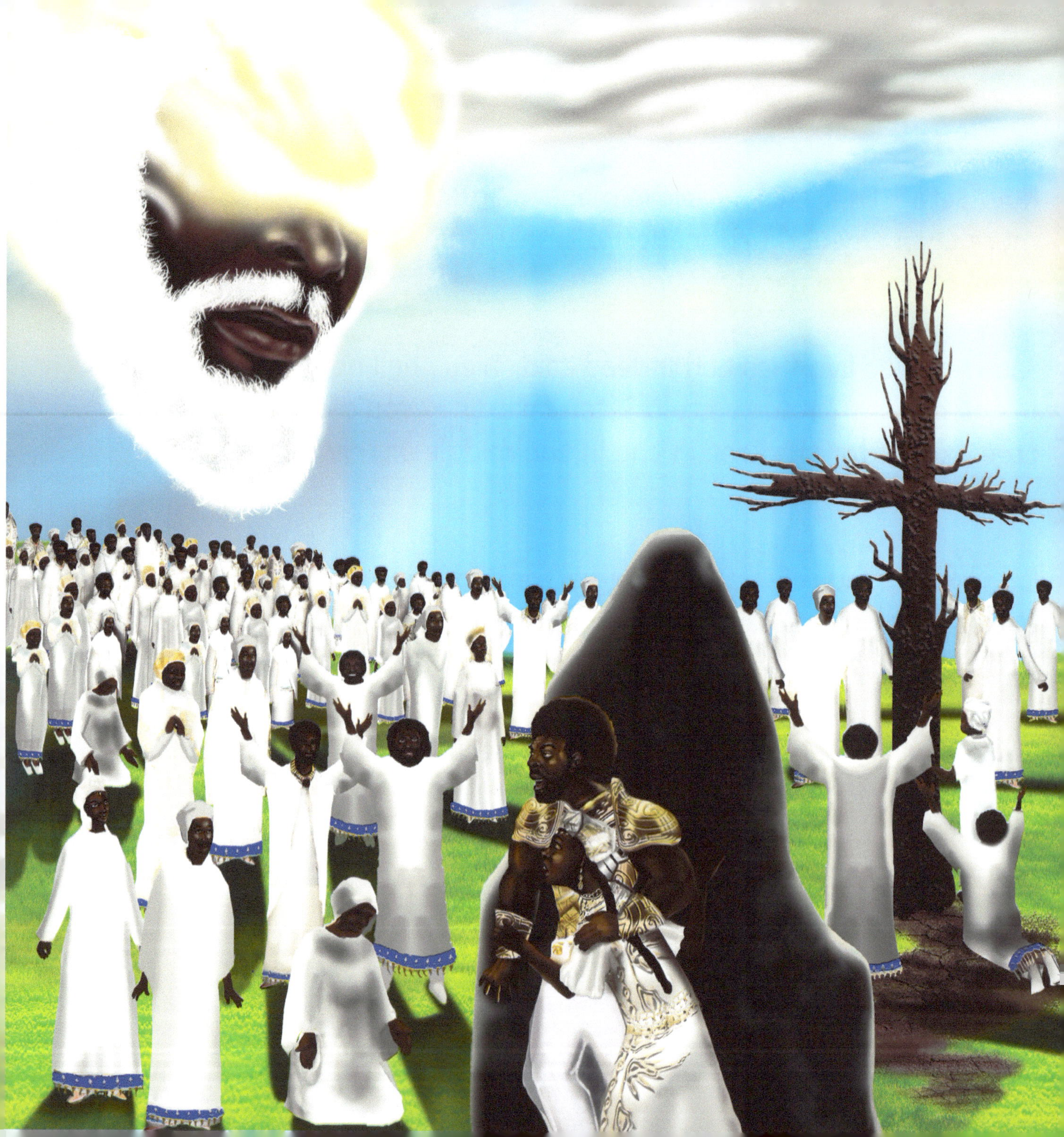

Then Adam and Eve heard the voice of the God in the garden and they hid themselves amongst their children in the garden.

God called to Adam and said, 'Where are you?'

Adam said, 'I heard Your voice in the garden and I was afraid because I had broken your commandments so I hid myself amongst our children in the garden.'

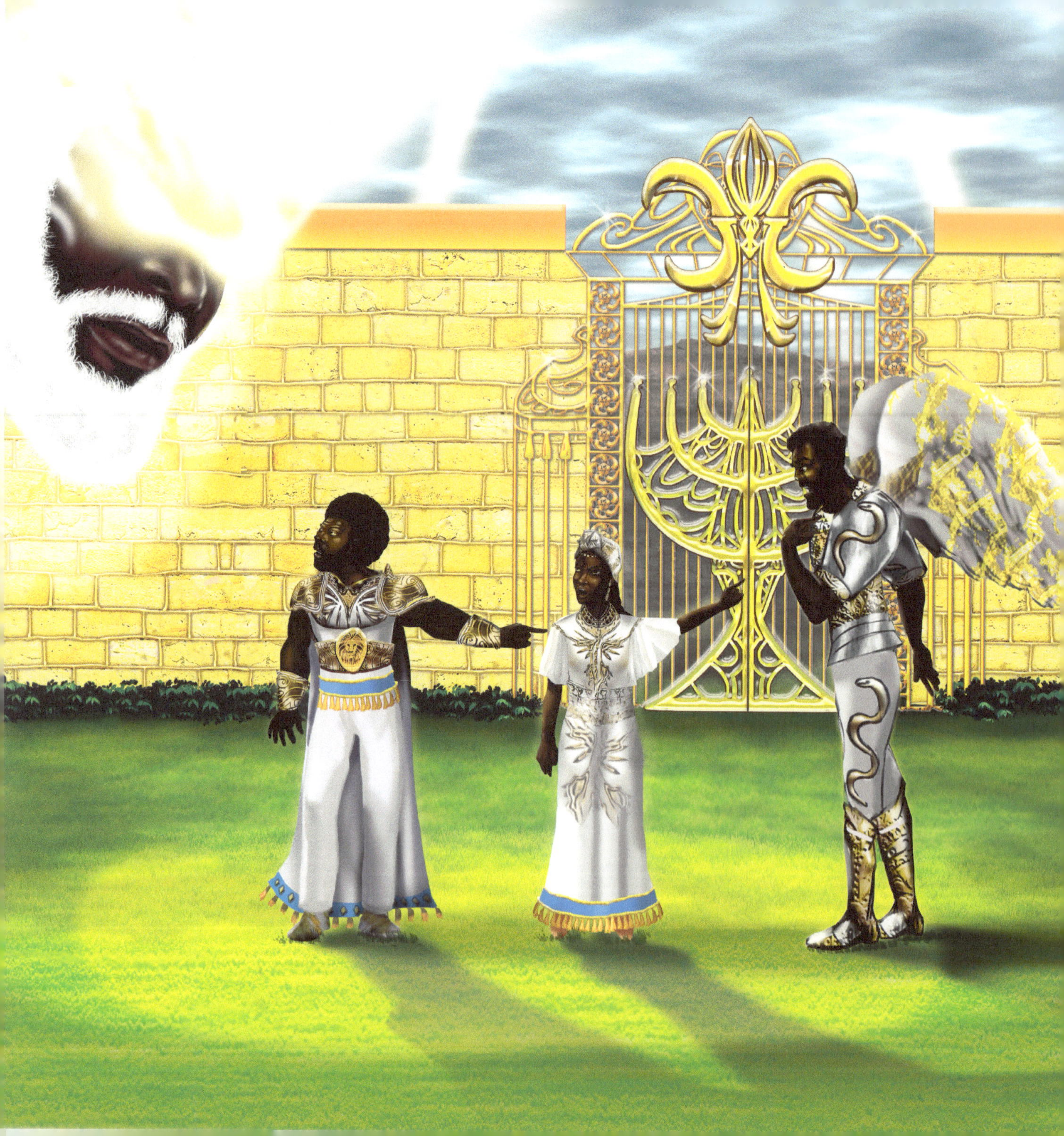

Adam said to God, 'The woman who You gave as my wife, she gave me of the tree, and I ate, and she taught me.'

God said to Eve, 'What is this you have done?' Eve told God that Satan had tricked her and she listened to him.

God said to Eve, 'In pain you shall bring forth children' and told her that her desire should be for her husband and not Satan.

God said to Adam, 'Because you have listened to the voice of your wife, and have eaten from the tree of which I commanded you, saying, "You should not eat of it": cursed is the ground for your sake: In toil you shall eat of it all the days of your life.'

God cursed the ground and now Man must work for their food and all things and by the sweat of hard work they will eat their food until they die.

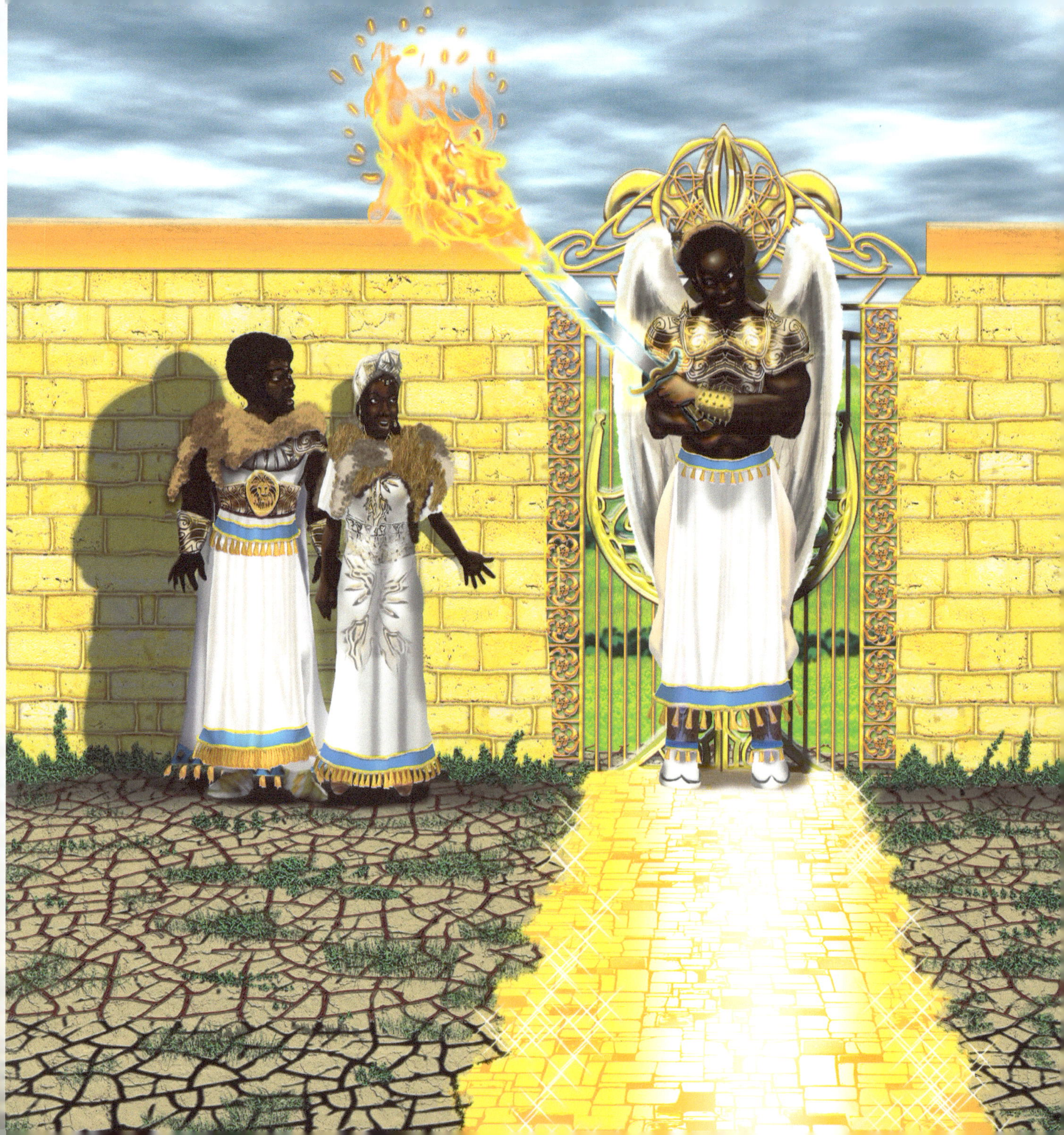

And God said, 'Behold, the man has become like one of Us, to know good and evil.'

So God drove Adam and Eve and all their children out of the Garden of Eden and placed them at the east of the garden. He placed an Angel with a flaming sword blocking every way to keep them away from the Tree of Life.

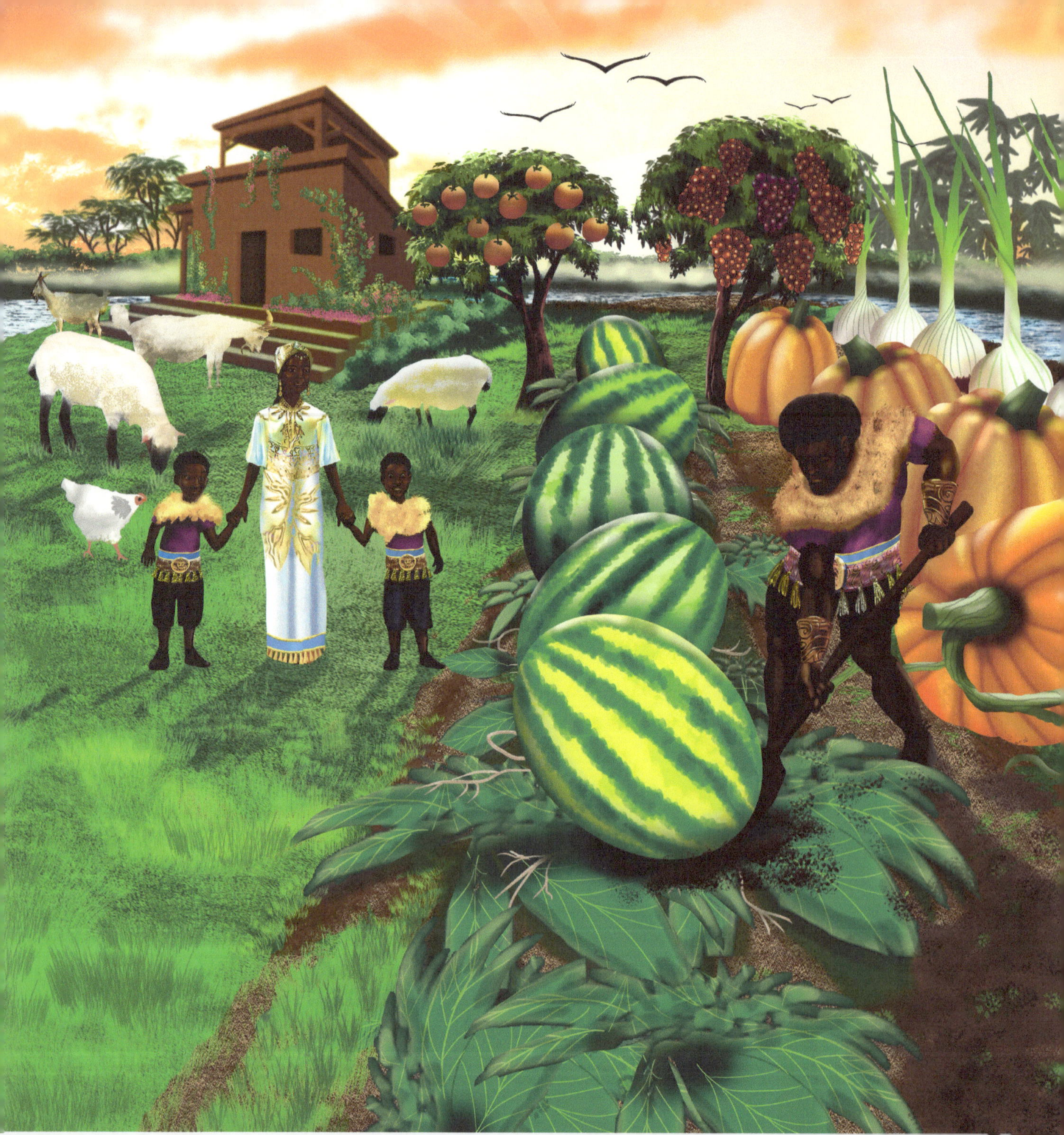

Adam's wife Eve gave birth to Cain and Eve said, 'I have acquired a man child from the Lord.' Then Eve gave birth to his brother, Abel. Abel grew up to be a keeper of sheep and Cain grew up to be a farmer and grow food from the ground.

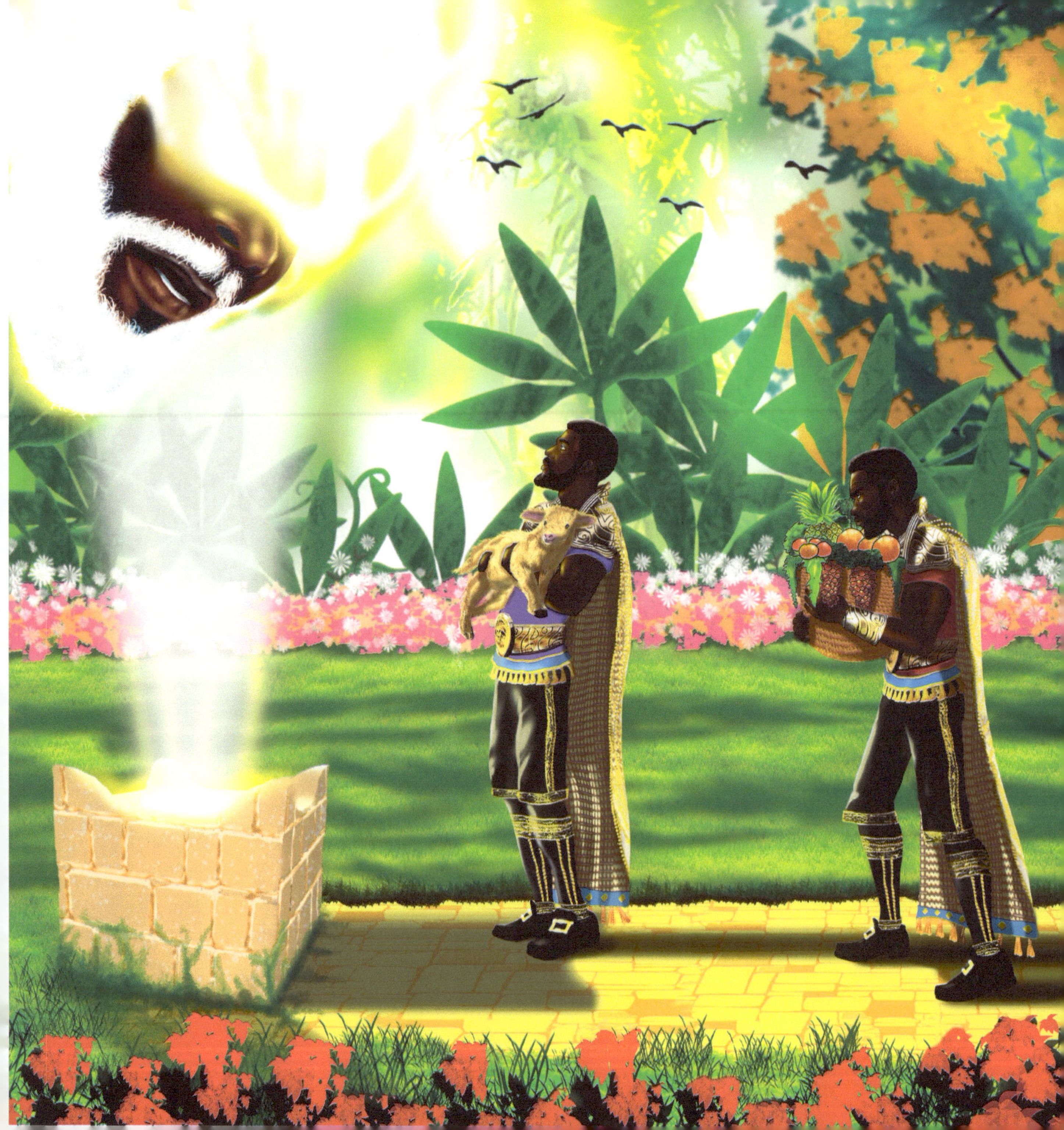

When Cain and Abel turned into men, they had to give a offering to God. Cain brought his fruits from the ground for an offering to God and Abel gave his first and the best of his sheep. God had respect for Abel and was delighted with his offering. But God had no respect for Cain's because he did not offer the best of fruits. This made Cain very angry and his face was sad.

And God said to Cain, 'if you would have kept my commandments to bring me the best of your offering, I would have accepted your offering. But if you break my commandments and sin then Satan will rule over you.'

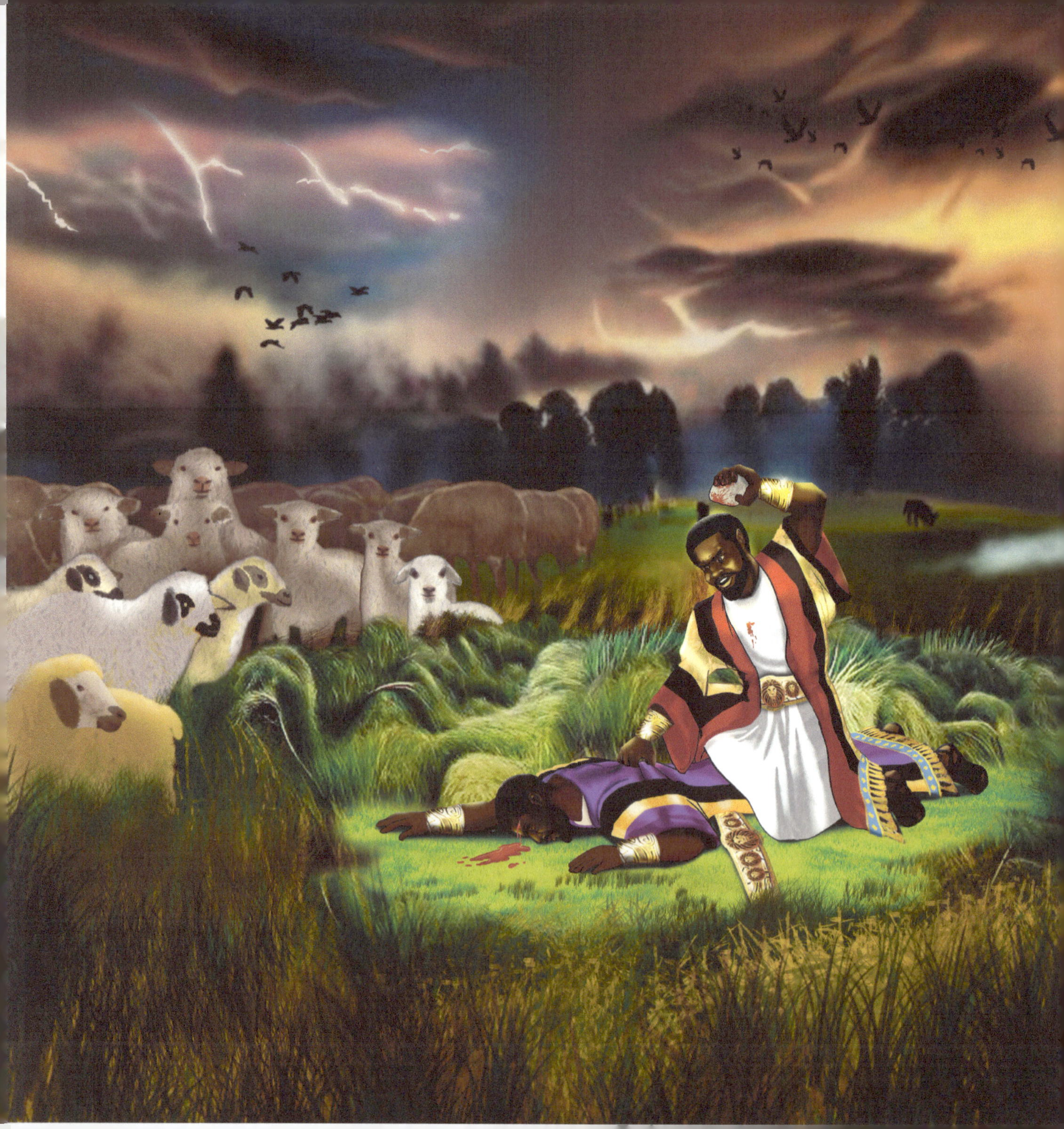

Some time later, Cain was talking to his brother Abel in the field. Cain was jealous and hated his brother because God had respect for Abel's offering and not his. So Cain rose up and killed his brother Abel.

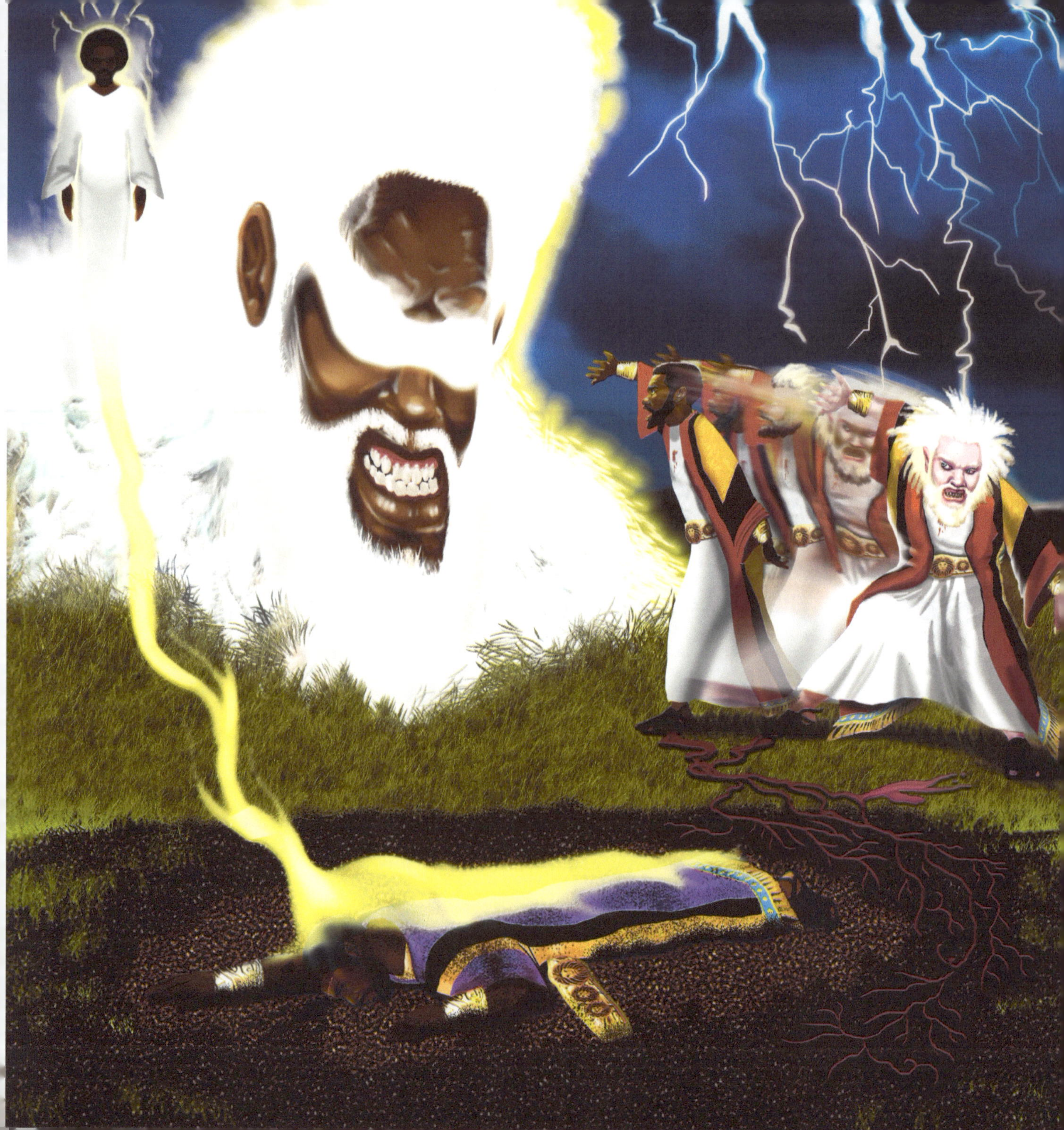

God said to Cain, 'Where is Abel your brother?' Cain said, 'I do not know. Am I my brother's keeper?' Then God said, 'What have you done? The voice of your brother's blood cries out to Me from the ground. Now you are cursed from the earth.' God told him that crops will no longer grow strong for him, and he will never be able to grow healthy food from the earth.

Cain killed his own brother, so God cursed Cain and his skin became white as snow so that wherever Cain went, people would know what he had done.

'A fugitive and vagabond you shall be on the earth,' said God. And by His hand, He made him a landless criminal. Cain said to God, 'My punishment is greater than I can bear! Surely You have driven me out this day from the face of the ground; I shall be hidden from Your face; I shall be a fugitive and a vagabond on earth.' Cain knew that everyone would see his skin would kill him because he had killed his brother which broke God's commandments.

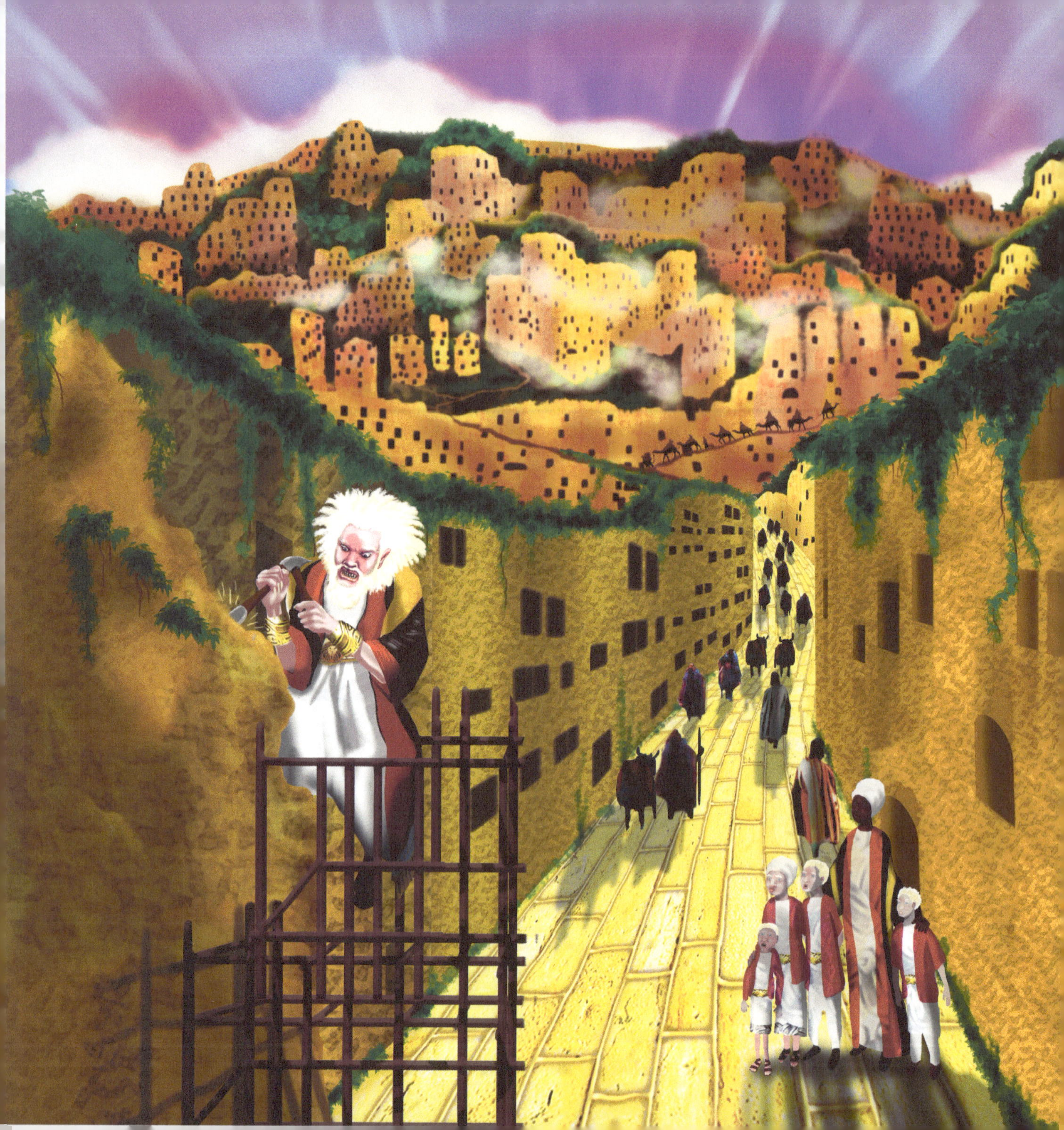

And Cain left the presence of God and lived in the Land of Nod on the east of Eden. Some time later, Cain met his wife and she gave birth to Enoch. Cain built a city and named it after his son Enoch. Cain and his wife had many children.

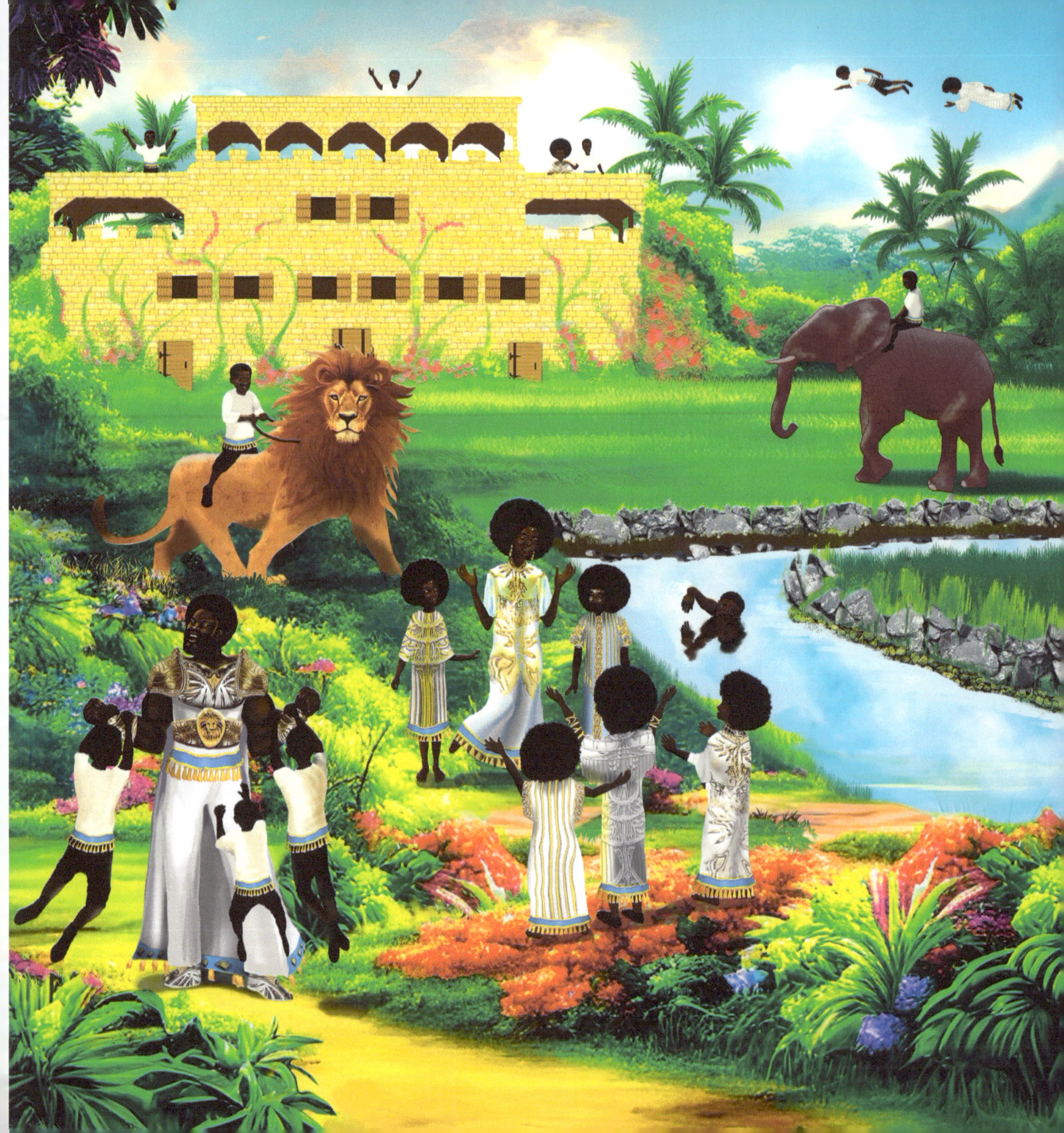

Adam's wife, Eve, gave birth to a son named Seth. Eve was so happy that God had given her another son after Cain killed Abel. Adam and Eve had many children, sons and daughters, and Adam lived 930 years and then he died.

Conscious Dreams
PUBLISHING

Transforming diverse writers into successful published authors

www.consciousdreamspublishing.com

authors@consciousdreamspublishing.com

Let's connect